Warning!

Before you read this book, you should know that snowboarding is dangerous. If you are not careful, and even sometimes if you are, you can break bones, including that hard skull that wraps up your brain. The safest thing to do is just to read this book in the comfort of your own bed at home. But if you plan to actually get up on a snowboard, protect yourself by taking some lessons, using the right equipment, always boarding with a buddy, and only doing tricks that you're ready for.

A WORD ABOUT HELMETS: Many of the pictures of snowboarders in this book show them without helmets. This is because snowboarding grew out of skiing, and skiers don't wear helmets. But leaving your head unprotected while snowboarding is a very bad idea. It's what you use to see, hear, eat, think, and talk with. You don't want to break it!

If you *do* go out and break your head, or any other part of your body or anyone else's body, don't blame National Geographic. We told you to be careful!

(Translation into legalese: Neither the publisher nor the author shall be liable for any bodily harm that may be caused or sustained as a result of conducting any of the activities described in this book.)

One of the world's largest nonprofit scientific and educational organizations, the NATIONAL GEOGRAPHIC SOCIETY was founded in 1888 "for the increase and diffusion of geographic knowledge." Fulfilling this mission, the Society educates and inspires millions every day through its magazine, books, television programs, videos, maps and atlases, research grants, the National Geographic Bee, teacher workshops, and innovative classroom materials. The Society is supported through membership dues, charitable gifts, and income from the sale of its educational products. This support is vital to National Geographic's mission to increase global understanding and promote conservation of our planet through exploration, research, and education.

For more information, please call 1-800-NGS LINE (647-5463) or write to the following address:
National Geographic Society
1145 17th Street N.W.
Washington, D.C. 20036-4688 U.S.A.
Visit the Society's Web site at www.nationalgeographic.com.

NATIONAL GEOGRAPHIC

EXTREME Sports

SNOWBOARD!

Your Guide to Freeriding, Pipe & Park, Jibbing, Backcountry, Alpine, Boardercross, and more

BY JOY MASOFF

Illustrations by Jack Dickason

NATIONAL GEOGRAPHIC

WASHINGTON, D.C.

What's Inside

Going Big

Just how big can a person go? Ask this boarder, who's about to deploy a parachute —a fitting end to a really radical run.

This is a book for dreamers...

...a book for anyone who has ever watched a snowboarder soaring through the air, or carving through deep powder on a steep, snowy cliff. . . .

This is a book of possibilities—a chance to discover all the reasons why snowboarding has become one of the hottest, hippest sports in history—and a chance to learn how to take your boarding to the next level.

This is a book of accomplishments—a celebration of the amazing feats of the world's best snowboarders. These are the tricks that leave us breathless, the spins that make us gasp, the grabs that leave us dazzled, and the victories that make us feel that anything is possible with a lot of hard work, determination, and a dream that won't quit.

This is a book that proves that if you really want to, you CAN fly!

Extreme Sports

Part One

Wild Rides

- Freeriding
- Backcountry
- In the Pipe
- Boardercross
- Alpine/Speed
- Jibbing
- Terrain Parks
- Sandboarding

So what's it gonna be?
A "big air" ride down the halfpipe?
A trip through the backcountry?
Head-to-head with a couple of buddies?
The choice is yours....

Stoked to Ride

You've been boarding a few times and now you're hooked on the awesome feeling of power and freedom you get when you ride the hills. Now it's time to take your riding to the next level.

Picture this. You're standing at the top of a mountain on a perfect winter day. Now what? Imagine zipping down that hill, going forward and then backward…sideways and upside down. Throw in a spin and a twist or two. Carve a cloud of snow. Be artistic and put together all sorts of different moves, or go for brute speed. A snowboarder can boldly go where no mere skier would dare.

A HIGHER LEVEL

Snowboarding is a "fast-learn" sport. It only takes the average person about a week to get the hang of it. The best piece of advice anyone can give a new snowboarder is, "Take lessons!" Sure, you can figure out things on your own. But in the meantime, you will fall a thousand times and probably learn the wrong way to do things. Besides, the sooner you learn the basics—how to stop, fall, and turn—the sooner you can move on to those monster "airs."

A MULTIPLE CHOICE QUIZ

Riding is all about choices. As you get better, and more in touch with your own style, it's fun to focus on all the things you can do with a snowboard. Do the boarders who can nail big-air tricks leave you drooling with envy? Or can you see yourself as a speed demon—someone who loves the thrill of going super-fast? Are you a daredevil who thinks that stair handrails were put on this Earth to ride down? Or are you the fearless sort, determined to find the most remote, unspoiled, steepest terrain imaginable?

DARING TO BE DIFFERENT

There are boarders who have ridden down Mt. Kilimanjaro. Boarders who ride New Mexico's giant sand dunes in the dead of summer wearing shorts and a big smile. Riders who have set speed records—reaching 95 miles an hour. Riders who can twist and turn their bodies in amazing ways. Now it's time for you to decide which style makes *your* heart beat just a little faster.

"GOTTA-KNOW" TERMS

BACKSIDE: The part of the snowboard where your heel rests, or the part of the mountain that your back faces.

FRONTSIDE: The part of the board where your toes are, or the part of the mountain that your chest faces.

HEELSIDE: The edge of the board where the heels of your boots end up.

GOOFY-FOOTED: Riding a snowboard with the right foot forward. Regular-footed boarders ride with the left foot forward.

FAKIE/SWITCH: Riding backwards. Also called switchstance. Doing a trick fakie makes it harder.

FRONT HAND: The hand closest to the nose(front) of the snowboard.

REAR HAND: The hand closest to the back (tail) of the snowboard.

SICK: Exceptionally awesome, as in "that deep powder was so sick!"

STICK: Another name for a snowboard. A really cool board would be a "sick stick." Also, to land without hopping as in "he really stuck that landing."

BAIL: To crash land.

Freeriding

No crowds. No judges. No starting gates.
No halfpipes and snarling snowcats. No
timers ticking away the seconds. Just
you and maybe a few buddies going
steep and deep on the mountain.

ne mountain, one rider, and an
anything-goes, laid-back kind of
attitude…that's freeriding. It's the soul of
boarding—a chance to mix it up as you make
your way down the slopes—with deep carved
turns, jumps and spins, frontsides and fakies.
Whatever you want, whenever you choose.

HEART AND SOUL

Freeriding is the core of snowboarding. You can freeride down a gentle slope, taking your time, carving slow, lazy turns. Or you can shoot down a sheer, vertical cliff, skimming off rocks and leaping onto fallen tree branches as you go. Freeriding is a definite state of mind—one that draws on every technical aspect of boarding.

DO IT YOUR WAY

Freeriding is all about your own personal style—drawing its cool moves and attitude from skateboarding and surfing, then putting its own special stamp on them. A freeride begins as you stand at the top of a run deciding what line you're going to take. "What can I jump off on the way down?" "That rock looks like it'd be great to smack with my tail." "Those rollers and knolls look awesome." Freeriding is about using the terrain to showcase your boarding skills.

WOOD WORKING

Riding in the woods is an extra thrill. Some boarders find areas they like and create their own artificial terrain parks by bending birch trees at the beginning of the winter and tying the branches to the ground to form rainbow-shaped arches. Then when the snows come, the trees freeze in the arched position—perfect for jibbing (see pages 22–23).

Johnny Noel jibs a tree trunk in the Vermont backcountry.

RIDING THE "POW"

Going off trail and riding in the woods where the snow has not been packed down is totally different from boarding in a resort area. And riding through deep powder, which boarders call POW, is a thrill! Here are some tips.

1. Stay centered over your board. Don't lean back too much. Keep it really loose and relaxed. Take a few deep breaths.

2. Ride in open areas the first few times. Try to find a place without too many obstacles in the way.

3. Don't turn as much or as often as you usually do. Try to master going straight first.

4. When you're feeling comfortable, try rocking gently from side to side. This will get you into your turn.

5. To send up a big plume of snow with each rock, give a sharp snap to your tail.

6. Don't be afraid of wiping out. Falling in powder is part of the fun.

Backcountry

Where do master freeriders go when they want to go extra-big? They say "bye-bye" to the lift lines. They skip the trips to the lodge for a cup of cocoa. Instead, they grab a shovel, a backpack, and an avalanche beacon and head off into the wilds to find a really awesome ride.

Backcountry boarding is not for the timid or the weak. But it is a thrill you'll never forget. It'll give you a taste of riding the way it was in the rugged pioneer days of snowboarding.

Maybe you'll end up zigzagging through a pine forest using the trees for slalom gates. Maybe you'll hike uphill for hours, then strap on your board for the ride of a lifetime down an untracked chute or over a snow-draped cornice. Any way you look at it, you'll love it.

LEAVING IT ALL BEHIND

Everything about boarding changes in the wilderness. The terrain is steeper, the trees taller, the obstacles bigger. And the only sound you'll hear is the hammering of your heart and the swish of your board through pure unspoiled snow. Riding in the backcountry is a rush, but it can be very dangerous.

FROM WIPEOUTS TO WHITEOUTS

Ski resorts groom their trails, packing the snow down with snowcats and tractors. The snow in the backcountry is different. You must respect its power. Avalanches—sudden rushes of massive amounts of snow—can bury and suffocate a person in minutes.

There are two kinds of avalanche. A sluff avalanche occurs when waves of snow roll across a hard-packed base. Experienced boarders can actually ride a sluff, hitting speeds of 60–70 mph—like skimming on ball-bearings. But they ride the sluffs only to get out of the way of the oncoming sea of snow.

More dangerous are slab avalanches. These occur when the snow pack fractures and a thick wall of snow starts sweeping downhill. A slab avalanche can take down an entire forest. It can kill in a matter of seconds. Being trapped beneath several feet of snow is like being trapped in concrete. You can't move, and you can't breathe.

An avalanche roars down a mountainside destroying everything in its path.

ROCKS…AND ROLL!

Here are some secrets from the pros for riding in the wild. Throw a few rocks in your backpack. Then, when you get to the place you want to ride, toss the rocks down one at a time and study the path they roll down. That will be the best route down for you. Rent a splitboard—a special snowboard that breaks apart to mimic skis so you can cross difficult terrain without having to carry snowshoes or crampons. And keep looking back up the hill to see if you've started any sluffs. If you have, get out of the way!

Ride with your heart and soul and get set to laugh out loud with pure joy!

DANGER: AVALANCHE!

1. Never EVER ride alone. Go with an experienced backcountry guide your first few times out and always ride with a buddy after you've become familiar with the terrain.

2. Pack a map and a compass as well as a plan for the day. Tell your family or friends exactly where you're going. Don't change your plans.

3. Make sure you have an avalanche kit with you—a folding shovel, a beacon, probe poles, and special charts for evaluating the snow quality. Learn how to use them.

4. Be prepared for sudden changes in the weather. Food and drink are absolute necessities in case you get stranded. An extra set of clothing is also a must-have.

In the Pipe

Imagine boarding up the side of a three-story building. Imagine being shot out of a cannon while riding a roller coaster.
Now, try riding the half and quarterpipes and find out what it feels like!

Back in the 1970s, skateboarders discovered the thrill of riding in drainage ditches and along empty swimming pool sides. When snowboards burst on the scene, people wanted the same thrills. But ski resort owners were afraid boarders would get in the way of skiers and banned them from their mountains. Folks had to search for a decent spot to ride. One of the first, and best, spots was built on the edge of a snow-covered garbage dump. Its fame soon spread and the legendary Tahoe City Pipe was born. Snowboarding the halfpipes became the new "in" thing!

BIGGER IS BETTER

A typical halfpipe is about 400–700 feet long and between 14 and 18 feet high. Monster pipes, called superpipes, are the next wave of pipe-riding, allowing riders to "go huge." Quarterpipes are mammoth—25–35 feet high and up to 50 feet wide. Some quarterpipes mimic ski jumps with a long steep approach that curls up at the end. Riders soar up to 30 feet above the coping (the edge of the pipe), sticking huge tricks.

IN THE AIR

A freestyler (another name for a pipe person) begins by "dropping in" the pipe, then moving down, crossing from one side to the other. Every approach to the top edge of the pipe is called a "hit." In competitions, a rider will try to get as many quality hits as possible. Too few, and the judges will be unimpressed. Too many tricks will make the rider go too slow, unable to get "big air." The balance between tricks and speed has to be exactly right.

This park features both a half and quarterpipe for twice the fun.

DROPPING IN

How can you get started? Try skateboarding and learn to work a skate halfpipe. Don't drop in the first few times you snowboard. Just cruise through the mouth of the pipe. When you're ready to try dropping in, follow the lines of those who've already ridden. Don't try to catch air at first. Ollie in sideways (see page 32–33), keep your knees bent, and try to reach the edge of the pipe. Study the other riders' moves.

TEN "SICK" PIPE MOVES

1. AIR-TO-FAKIE: Approach the wall riding forward, go up, then come down backward.

2. ALLEY-OOP: A 180-degree spin heading up the wall.

3. ANDRECHT: A rear-handed, backside handplant while doing a front hand grab.

4. CAB: Any trick that starts fakie on your switch frontside wall, while spinning frontside.

5. CRIPPLER AIR: Approach the wall riding forward, get airborne, rotate 90 degrees, flip over in the air, rotate another 90 degrees, and land riding forward.

6. SAD PLANT: A handplant with the front leg straightened.

7. A 720: The rider approaches the wall riding forward, rotates around twice, and lands riding fakie. It can also be done switchstance.

8. McTWIST: Approach the wall riding forward, get airborne, rotate one and a half times (540 degrees) in a backside direction while doing a front flip. Land forward. Pair it with a **McEGG**—an invert with a front handplant, followed by a 540-degree rotation in a backside direction—for a true happy meal!

9. BACKSIDE RODEO: Also called a Michaelchuck (after its inventor Mike Michaelchuck). An inverted/off-axis 540-degree turn over the rear shoulder.

10. POP TART: Airing from fakie to forward with no rotation.

Boardercross

The seconds count down, and your heart beats faster. Around you, five other riders shift nervously, slapping their boards onto the snow to clear off any ice. Finally, the gate springs open, and you're out and off…six bodies hurtling through space.

Who will make it to the bottom first?

Boarder X, or Boardercross, is one of the hottest rides around—a wild push that pits up to six boarders against each other and one mountain. First one across the finish line wins. It's that simple. There are no clocks. No judges. Sometimes the course is a beauty. Other times it's a mess. But one thing is certain. Boardercross is the hottest thing to hit snowboarding in a long time.

HEAD TO HEAD COMBAT

Imagine a motocross track, cover it with snow, and you have a good idea of what a boardercross course looks like—table, gap, and triple jumps…berms and whoop-dee-doos. When riders hit a "whoops"—a series of artificial big bumps—just about anything goes, including their knees from time to time. Boardercross can be really tough on a body.

Got guts of iron, nerves of steel, and solid snowboarding skills? Here's how boardercross works.

ON COURSE FOR GLORY

Typically there are anywhere from 24 to 48 racers starting in a pro event. They are divided into groups of six riders who compete against each other in heats. The top three finishers in each heat move into the next round.

It's wild out on the course. Bodies flying, people falling. Sometimes the strategy is to bump into another rider to throw him or her off balance. But it sure is exciting to watch!

TIPS FROM THE PROS

1. Know the basics inside and out. Don't try to handle a boardercross course until you know your stuff. The best boardercrossers are as comfortable on their boards as they are on their two feet.

2. Be in tip-top shape. Lift weights to keep your upper body as strong as your legs.

3. Stay focused. Be aware of what's happening around you, from that rider who's breathing down your neck to the triple that's just ahead.

4. Don't go all out in the early heats. You'll run out of steam by the time you make it to the finals. But *do* go all out when the starting gate bursts open. An early lead is a definite advantage.

5. Always "slip" the course first. That means slowly sliding down sideways, studying each jump and turn. Try to memorize the course.

6. Ready to give it a go? There are courses at many of the bigger resorts with real starting gates and timed runs.

On your mark, get stoked, GO! These Boarder X racers are just coming over a whoop-dee-doo.

Alpine/ Speed

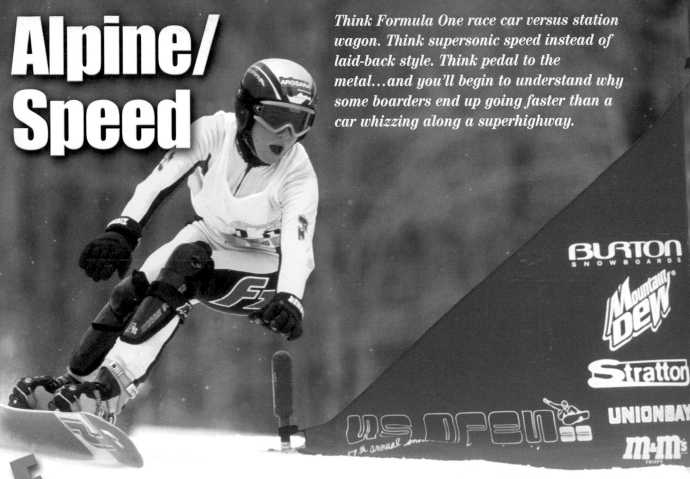

Think Formula One race car versus station wagon. Think supersonic speed instead of laid-back style. Think pedal to the metal...and you'll begin to understand why some boarders end up going faster than a car whizzing along a superhighway.

For some snowboarders, the thought of spinning, grabbing, and catching air leaves them cold. They love the feeling of free-falling, the adrenaline-rush of hurtling down a steep slope at Mach speed. They're alpine boarders, and this is their side of the snowboard.

They have learned how to defy the laws of gravity, to push their bodies almost level with the snow. They can cut their edges at really radical angles to go even faster. And they have been clocked at upwards of 90 miles an hour.

DEFYING GRAVITY

Have you ever followed a motorcycle down a winding country road? Have you noticed how the biker leans into each of the curves? Alpine boarders do the same thing, dipping low as they carve deep S-turns down the slopes. The result is an incredible feeling of weightlessness. Imagine riding your own personal roller coaster all day long (one where you *always* have a seat in the front row). That's how one rider described boarding alpine style.

STIFFER, HARDER, FASTER

Forget soft, comfy boarding boots. Forget rideboards that are compact and spinnable. If you want to go fast—really, really fast— you need to start with special equipment. Stiff boots, made like regular ski boots, are a must. So is an extra-long, super-rigid board. And you'll definitely need a helmet 'cause you're about to take off like a rocket.

The stiff boards, shaped into an hourglass by deep sidecuts, allow alpinists to ride almost parallel to the snow. The tail is flat for more edge contact. Often, the rider will be balanced on the thinnest edge of the board—a sliver of metal not much wider than an ice-skate blade.

If a ride on a freestyle board is like riding on a pony, a ride on an alpine board is like saddling up a wild mustang. You really have to have superb skills to be able to handle one.

Bottoms up! A good alpiner is usually on the edge of the board.

A RACE TO THE FINISH

If you like to go really fast, you'll probably want to try racing. Here are some frequently asked questions about alpine boarding.

1. WHY DO YOU NEED SPECIAL EQUIPMENT?
If you are serious about riding for speed, you have to get the proper equipment. Rigid boots will help you lean deeper into the turns for longer periods of time. Stiffer boards can hold an edge better and won't chatter (rattle) at high speeds.

2. WHAT'S A RACE LIKE?
Riders have to move through a series of triangular gates nicknamed "stubbies." These gates are shaped differently from skiing slalom gates since boarders lean so much further into their turns than conventional skiers.

3. WHAT'S THE BEST THING ABOUT RACING?
Great friendships develop between riders on the racing circuit. They love hanging out with one another and, even though they might be rivals on the course, they're the best of buddies when the race is over. And best of all, they get to travel all over the world doing what they love best—snowboarding!

Jibbing

Snowboarding down a steep mountain is cool. Snowboarding over trees, rocks, rails, and cars is even cooler—if you have the skills to pull it off.

Stairs, fences, outdoor furniture, roofs, tree stumps, and branches. What do they have in common? They're heaven to jibbers—snowboarders who love to glide, ride, and jump over all sorts of natural and artificial obstacles.

SNOWBOARDING CITY-SIDE

Jibbers are a pretty extreme group. They don't even need a mountain to ride on. Dedicated jibbers in the heart of a big city can shovel their way to boarding heaven. They seek out flights of stairs, railings, and snow-covered cars. Garbage cans, rolled on their sides and covered with snow, make great jumps. Out in the woods, the jibbing targets are bigger. Trees, from stumps to fallen logs, provide a wild ride. Rocks and boulders provide great jumping-off points.

JIB MUST-HAVES

Grab a helmet. Get a shovel. Pack some food and drink. Now you're ready to start jibbing. Terrain parks are the best places to get started. There are all sorts of pipe railings, from rainbow rails, which curve, to rails set at right angles. There are tabletops and platforms to choose from and no one will yell at you for riding. (See pages 24–25 for more.) After you've mastered the basics, try getting creative, such as coming off the rails into a fakie. If you're jibbing in the city, respect private property. Scout around and look for good places to ride before it snows.

WARNING! DANGER!

Rough terrain can ruin a snowboard. You should always be careful about slamming your board around. The pressure of your body can snap the board in half if you get too aggressive. Think like a cat and ride like a floating feather.

HOW TO RIDE A RAIL

Rail-riding is awesome, but it takes practice. And it takes something even more important—a helmet! Don't even think of trying a trick without protecting your skull. There's nothing remotely cool about brain damage! NEVER attempt any trick until you are a really confident rider.

1. Start your approach towards the rail. Don't go too fast or too slow.

2. See pages 32–33 and learn how to ollie. Then, ollie up high enough to get up and over the rail.

3. Extend your legs and plant your board on the rail.

4. Align the board. Choose perpendicular for a rail slide or go parallel for a 50/50 grind. There are other variations, but these are the most popular.

5. Balance lightly on your board. Let gravity carry you. Settle in gently.

6. Be prepared for a change of speed as your board settles into the slide. Metal will go faster than snow. Wood feels slower.

7. As you come to the end of the rail, hop up slightly, then straighten the board out and land riding forward.

Terrain Parks

If you like jibbing, you'll love the tricks and treats that await you at the newest thing to hit boarding— special playgrounds! After all, going downhill isn't all there is to snowboarding.

Mention whales and you probably think of the ocean. Mention whales to a die-hard snowboarder and watch his or her eyes light up. From super-slippery rails to whale-sized mounds of snow, parks are where the fun is.

24

ALL-TERRAIN VEHICLES

At a terrain park, your snowboard will take you over some pretty awesome obstacles. You can leap over tables, whalebacks, spines, quarterpipes, hips, pyramids, step-ups, funboxes, and, of course, those radical rails. Terrain parks were inspired by skateboarding parks. And the neatest part is, landing in the snow doesn't hurt nearly as much as landing on asphalt.

BONKING

Terrain parks are the perfect spot to practice bonking. What's a bonk? It's a slap of the board against an obstacle. As the board hits a hard surface it makes a "bonk" sound. It's definitely a really sick move. To bonk something, ollie-up (see page 32), then push one leg down as you go over the object, tapping your board against it. Nose bonks are a slap with the front of your board. Tail bonks are...yup...you guessed it!

FROM FUNBOXES TO SPINES

What will you find in a terrain park? Tabletops look like tables with a kicker (a little ramp) leading up and a landing slope coming off the back. Spines are two small quarterpipes set back to back. Hips are similar to tabletops but with a diagonal approach. Funboxes are made of wood with a plastic top, perfect for bonking. Step-ups are like tabletops, except the landing is *higher* than the table. And for all you cetacean lovers, whales are really huge mounds of snow.

SLIDE GUIDE

Grinding or sliding is awesome. There are six basic grinding moves to master. Here's the countdown.

1. 50/50: Aim your snowboard parallel with the railing. This is the best grind to start with since it's almost impossible to catch an edge.

2. ROCK 'N' ROLL GRIND: The opposite of the 50/50. Your board is perpendicular to the rail with the rail right in between your feet.

3. SMITH GRIND: Start with a rock 'n' roll, then scoot your nose lower and more forward on the rail. Getting a little tougher, huh?

Rockin' and Rollin' on a railin' is really righteous.

4. NOSE SLIDE: A rock 'n' roll with the rail between your front foot and the nose.

5. TAIL SLIDE: Another variation of a rock 'n' roll, this time with the rail between your back foot and your board's tail.

6. FIVE-O GRIND: Pulling the equivalent of a snowboard wheelie on the rail. This is done from a 50/50 position.

(See page 23 for the basics of rail-riding.)

Sandboarding

What do furniture polish and sand have to do with snowboarding? For a die-hard group of riders, summer is simply an opportunity to ride a different type of mountain.

Summer's here. It's hotter than you-know-what outside. Time to pack your board away? Uh-uh. Time to head for the dunes. For some hard-core boarders, sand is even more fun than snow.

SNOWBOARDING WITHOUT SNOW

For the past few years boarders have flocked to a country in Africa called Namibia. There are no mountains there. But there's plenty of sand. The highest dunes in the world are in Namibia—some over 1,000 feet high—and this remote spot has become the sandboarding capital of the world. Other places offer cliffs of sand, too. Every continent except Antarctica offers amazing sandboarding spots.

Now, for those of you unable to jet off to Africa, there are 20 states in the U.S. where you can board on sand. Most of the dunes are in southern California and the Southwest, many at national and state parks and recreation areas. There may be some restrictions due to the delicate ecosystems, so check with the parks before downing those dunes.

SAND! MAN!

Sandboarding will give you a slower ride than snowboarding. Longer, carving turns rule. If you try shorter cutbacks, you'll end up on your butt with a mouthful of sand. The toughest part of sandboarding is the lack of chair lifts. Every ride is followed by a huffing, puffing hike back up to the top. If you've ever walked in ankle deep sand, you know how hard that is! Sand dunes near the ocean are best, since the moisture from the sea helps pack the sand more firmly. And early morning will offer up the best rides, before the sun has sucked up the moisture.

FORGET SANDCASTLE CONTESTS

Sandboarding competitions offer the same thrills that rule on snow with the same spins, flips, and grabs along with the usual style and flair.

There are competitions held all over the world in duel slalom, big air, freestyle, and distance jumping. As the word gets out, more and more boarders realize that summer doesn't mean the end of hitting the slopes. Sandboarding will just keep getting bigger and better. And best of all, your fingers will never, ever get cold!

POINTERS FROM THE PROS

1. You can probably use your regular snowboard on sand provided you find a dune that is steep enough. Remember, sand rides slower.

2. Don't use snow wax on your base. Scrape off all the old wax before you ride sand. Some riders swear by Lemon Pledge furniture polish! Wax on the edges is a must.

3. Ride farther back on the board—kind of like riding in powder. This lifts the board tip up. More air passes under the board, and you'll get a zippier ride.

4. Wear sunglasses or goggles. Sand in your eyes is definitely painful.

Extreme Sports

Part Two

The Moves

You know how and where you can ride.
Now, learn how to put together
some smooth moves.
Grab with style. Spin with speed.
And look really cool!

Ripping with Style

Your board can take you to some pretty amazing places. But not only can you ride it slopeside, you can turn it into a flying carpet.

If you've ever watched snowboarding on TV you've seen the big, bust-a-gut moves—the oh-my-gosh-how-did-they-do-that-and-survive jumps and spins. What does it take to pull those kinds of moves off?

BONK AND GRIND

If you've reached the point where riding your board is as easy as walking, it's time to push on to the next level. But even if you still move like Frankenstein, it's fun to learn all about the moves being done slopeside these days. Whether it's spinning, sliding, flipping, grinding, or bonking—skateboard-influenced moves and the new, bigger pipes have definitely upped the quality of the tricks being done.

GETTING A JUMP ON GETTING STARTED

Nobody simply straps on a board after a few lessons and jibs a rail in the park or ollies a tree stump perfectly. Understand that the riders hitting these big tricks have fallen ten thousand times. They have spent hours every day on trampolines, building up their muscles, getting comfortable with their moves. Then they have headed off to the pipes or the parks or the mountainsides a hundred times and crashed over and over and *over* again. It takes patience, practice, and then a little more practice to pull off a big move. You must be completely dedicated.

HOW "HIP" ARE YOU?

You might think that your legs are the most important body part in snowboarding. But to really move with flash and dash, you need to think about a few other parts of your body, especially your hips and shoulders. Remember these two things!

1. Your shoulders move your hips, and your hips move the board.
2. Your shoulders and your head are responsible for every move you make while boarding.

THE SNOWBOARDER'S MOTTO

If you were lucky enough to have a coach, your coach would tell you this:

Fear creates doubt.
Doubt leads to failure.

Remember this as you start to learn new tricks. Practice over and over again when you're learning something new. If you're afraid to do something, don't even try. But if you're ready, go for your moves without holding back or hesitating.

Ollies & Nollies

Before you can dazzle the crowds with your monster grabs you have to become one with your board—to learn to feel the way the edges work as you move through the snow.

Just as you spread butter on a piece of bread, you have to learn how to "butter" the mountain with your board. Keep that image in your mind and experiment with using your board to "spread" the snow on the mountain.

OLLIE-UP

The most important move you can learn is the ollie (see page 33). It's the basis of just about every jump and spin you'll ever do. It's best to learn to do an ollie while riding your board on level ground. In fact, the trickiest part of pulling off an ollie is landing it flat. To build your confidence, try scooching your board while you're flatlanding. A scooch is a little slide of the board from side to side, kind of like a pendulum on a clock.

Jibbers who ride stair-railings use the ollie to get up onto the rails. Halfpipers start many of their moves with an ollie to get height on their jumps. You can ollie up, then twist your upper body in the opposite direction from your legs for a cool-looking shifty. Nollies are simply ollies done in reverse. Both are easy-to-learn, cool-to-do moves.

A TIP FROM THE PRO

Practice your ollie motion at home by hopping from foot to foot. Lift each knee as high as you can at the same time you hop up. Do this a few hundred times, until you have a smooth motion to your moves. That's an ollie!

ROCK ONTO YOUR BACK LEG

Put all your weight on your backside leg until the tip of the board starts to lift off the ground.

JUMP OFF YOUR BACK FOOT

Put some spring into that jump. You'll want to pull that backside knee up toward your chest.

PULL UP YOUR KNEE

As soon as you bring your back-leg knee up, quickly snap up your front-leg knee. Your board should lift up off the ground completely.

LEARN TO NOLLIE

Once you have the ollie motion down pat, do it in reverse. Rock onto your front leg, jump up off the front leg, pull up the back leg, then come down flat.

Practice until you can land the board flat. You don't ever want to come down on your tip or your tail.

Basic Grabs

You gotta grab if you want to be a star in the pipe. But which grab is which? If you're not sure what the difference is between a mute and a method, look no further. Here's how to do all the most common grabs.

Learning to grab will definitely make you look extra-hip. And not only will grabbing make you feel stoked, it will help make you a better boarder. With the board closer to your body, you will become more compact. Curled up in a tight ball, you can stay airborne longer and fly higher, with more stability.

Use the strength in your legs to bring your board up to your body instead of reaching down to make your grabs.

This boarder is showing off a boned front leg.

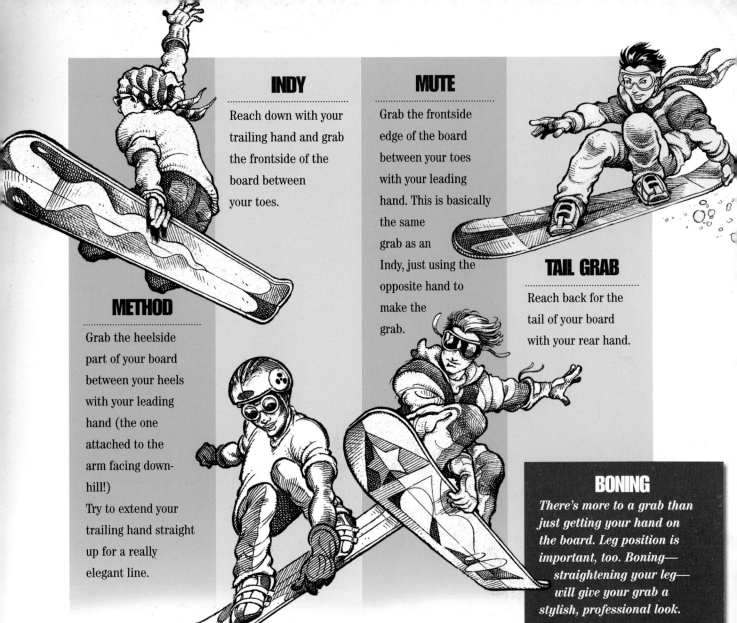

INDY

Reach down with your trailing hand and grab the frontside of the board between your toes.

MUTE

Grab the frontside edge of the board between your toes with your leading hand. This is basically the same grab as an Indy, just using the opposite hand to make the grab.

TAIL GRAB

Reach back for the tail of your board with your rear hand.

METHOD

Grab the heelside part of your board between your heels with your leading hand (the one attached to the arm facing down-hill!)
Try to extend your trailing hand straight up for a really elegant line.

BONING

There's more to a grab than just getting your hand on the board. Leg position is important, too. Boning—straightening your leg—will give your grab a stylish, professional look.

35

Tough Grabs

Time to take it up a notch. Time to see what you're really made of. You'll need a strong back, swingy hips, springy knees, and a whole lot of nerve. Hitting these grabs is a bit like playing a game of TWISTER in mid-air. Wild!

A perfect arch of the back or thrust of the hips is almost as important as where you put your hands.

Whenyou can pull off a perfect mute or method grab—when you're comfortable boning a leg and extending an arm, you're ready to push it a little harder. Grabs that require you to arch your body or reach around or through your legs are the next step up the snowboarding ladder.

36

NUCLEAR AIR

Reach across the front of your body with your rear hand and grab the heel edge in front of the front foot.

WALT AIR

Use your front hand to grab the heel edge near the tail. This is always done as a backside trick.

SEATBELT

The front hand reaches across the body (just like a car's seatbelt) and grabs the tail. Try to bone the front leg, too.

CRAIL

Grab the toe edge with your rear hand in front of the front foot. When you can do that, try to bone the rear leg.

DID YOU KNOW?

If you bone your front leg it's called a nose bone. A boned back leg is called a tail bone. Grabs are sorted into two types: frontside and backside grabs depending on the direction you're going.

The Grab Bag

There's no end to the possibilities when it comes to grabbing. Here are the most devilish moves around. See if you can figure out how to do them. But try them on dry ground first!

nce you've mastered the tough grabs, you'll be ready to take on the toughest grabs. These involve complicated hand positions and lots and lots of major attitude—back arched, legs boned, arms extended. You'll need really big air to buy yourself the time you need to hit these grabs.

INVENT A GRAB!

All grabs involve four things— your hands and your feet. There are countless combos of moves— toe edge, heel edge, leading hand or trailing hand, tail or tip, even the sides of your feet. Can you think of some new combos?

CHICKEN SALAD AIR

Your rear hand reaches between the legs and grabs the heel edge between the bindings. The front leg is boned, and the wrist rotates inward to make the grab.

CANADIAN BACON AIR

Use your rear hand to reach behind your rear leg and grab the toe edge between the bindings. The rear leg should be boned.

FLYING SQUIRREL

Bend your knees and grab the heel edge of the board with both hands. Front hand next to your front foot, rear hand next to your rear foot.

LIEN AIR

Grab the heel edge with your front hand and lean your body out over the nose. (Lien is Neil spelled backwards—named after the move's inventor, Neil Blender.)

SWISS CHEESE AIR

The rear hand reaches between your legs, goes behind the front leg, and grabs the heel edge in front of the front foot. Of course, you'll want to bone the back leg.

TAIPAN AIR

The front hand reaches behind the front foot and grabs the toe edge between the bindings. The front knee is then bent to kneel on the board—actually touching it.

SPAGHETTI AIR

Reach between your legs with your rear hand and snake it behind your front leg to grab your toe edge in front of the front foot. Try to bone your back leg.

STALEMASKY AIR

Use your front hand to reach between your legs and grab the heel edge between your bindings. Try to bone your front leg.

STALE FISH

Using your rear hand, grab the heel edge behind the rear leg and between the bindings. Try to bone the front leg.

ROAST BEEF AIR

The rear hand reaches between the legs, grabbing the heel edge between the bindings. The rear leg is boned.

Spinning Jumps

You're high in the air, your body coiled tightly. The clouds are under your feet, and the trees are growing upside down. The world whizzes by—blurry and beautiful. You've just uncorked a mega spin!

Sniffing your armpit and doing a twisting jump might not seem like they have much in common. But the best riders out there know better. Once you feel confident taking off from a jump, can land soundly, and know how to do a variety of grabs, you might want to start dreaming about putting a new twist into your snowboarding. From a simple 180 to a wild 1080—from a rip-your-heart-out McTwist to a gut-curling Rodeo—spinning jumps are what make superstars out of snowboarders.

SPIN CITY

Balls can spin in a lot of different directions—round and round, sideways, and "head over heels."

Your body can do the same things. The awesome jumps you see riders pulling as they hit the coping on the pipes or the top of a jump are based on the number of times their bodies rotate and in which direction they spin.

AERIAL ADVENTURES

An inverted aerial is any move where the rider is in the air and upside down. There are all sorts of inverted tricks based on the number of spins, from a 180 (halfway around) to a 1080 (three full revolutions). And just like the grabs, there are a ton of different variations of each. But be warned: Spinning jumps are awesome to watch but extremely dangerous to do. In many ski areas they are illegal. If you're seriously interested in learning how to pull off an aerial, it's best to start by training on a big trampoline (see pages 62–63 for some basic "tramp" training tips).

Any which way but up. Flipping off a jump takes a strong stomach and even stronger muscles.

FLIPPING YOUR LID

It's cool to watch a competition and know what moves the riders are hitting. These are some of the sickest, slickest spins around. You've already read about Cripplers, McTwists, and Rodeos on page 17. Here are some more cool moves.

HAAKON FLIP: An inverted switch 720 (2 spins)—usually done in the halfpipe. After a fakie approach, the rider rotates in the backside direction upside down. Named for Terje Haakonson—a true boarding genius.

MISTY FLIP: An inverted backside 540 (1 1/2 spins) done off a plain jump instead of the halfpipe with a forward approach and a fakie landing. If you do this trick in the halfpipe, it's a McTwist.

RODEO FLIP: A spectacular inverted frontside 540. Hit the jump takeoff, do a backflip, and land riding fakie.

There are all sorts of variations for these based on the number of rotations and the direction of takeoff and landing. But one thing is sure—they're all amazing to watch!

Competition

- Who's in Charge
- Extreme Games
- The Olympics

You can jump higher,
twist faster, handplant longer.
You can outrun the wind.
But are you ready to face off
against the best snowboarders
in the world?

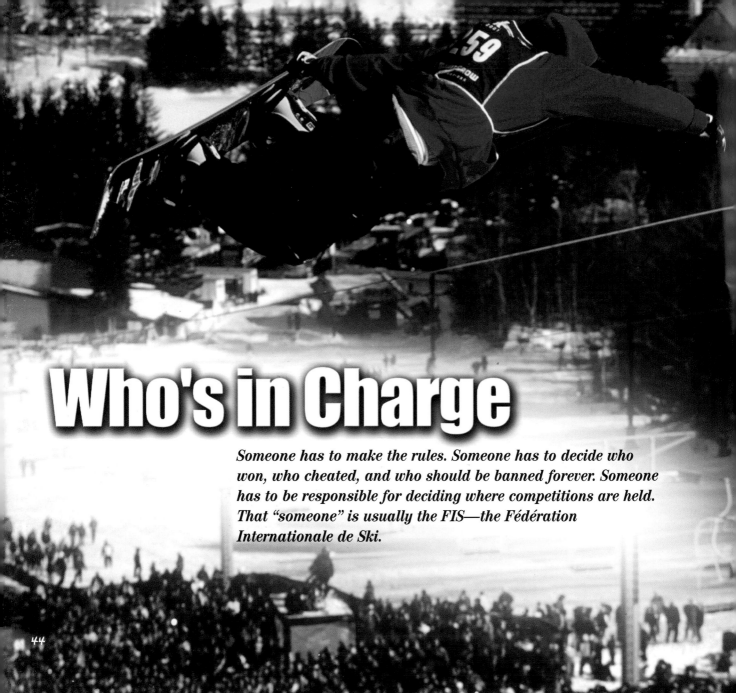

Who's in Charge

Someone has to make the rules. Someone has to decide who won, who cheated, and who should be banned forever. Someone has to be responsible for deciding where competitions are held. That "someone" is usually the FIS—the Fédération Internationale de Ski.

For an elite group of riders, snowboarding is more than just fun. It's how they earn a living. And whenever there is money and fame involved, things tend to get complicated. Everyone agrees that someone has to be in control—to run and organize the competitions, to make the rules, to provide and train the judges, to keep track of who won what, and to discipline people who break the rules. But who?

KING OF THE HILL

The International Ski Federation—Fédération Internationale de Ski—is known throughout the world as the FIS. It was established on February 2, 1924, during the very first modern Olympic Games in Chamonix, France. Fourteen nations joined. Today, over one hundred National Ski Associations make up the membership of the FIS. What does the FIS do? It organizes world competitions, writes the rules, and disciplines any athlete who breaks those rules. But notice the word "ski." Snowboarders felt lost in the shuffle. They wanted their own organization.

THE ISF—FOR BOARDERS ONLY

The International Snowboard Federation (ISF) was created for snowboarders by snowboarders. They, too, run competitions, and many athletes prefer the ISF events. The folks who run ISF competitions are committed to making sure the courses are in really good shape. They often offer more prize money and attract larger crowds. The atmosphere at an ISF event tends to be more festive, and boarders love the free-spirited feeling.

A WINNER IS BORN

Let's pretend you've been riding a while, and you can pull off a slew of super-sick jumps. Everyone says you're really hot. Now what?

1. SPEAK TO SOMEONE AT YOUR LOCAL RESORT. Find out if they have racing programs, pipe or park competitions. Many do. Start competing.

2. JOIN A GROUP such as the United States Snowboard Association. They sponsor events all across the country. Check online to see if there are any competitions in your area.

3. GET A SPONSOR. Your local board shop is a good place to start. When you've won a few races and gotten your picture in the paper a few times, you can contact a snowboard company and ask if they'd like to sponsor you. They might give you free equipment or pay you a small sum of money to use their gear. Send photos or a video of yourself nailing some impressive tricks. And always approach them in writing first. Don't call!

5. JOIN THE ISF OR THE FIS. At some point, if you are really serious about boarding, you will need to join one. If you want to be an Olympian, you must compete in official FIS events to earn enough Olympic points to qualify.

Extreme Games

"I'm faster than you." "I can spin more." "I can get bigger air." Everyone wants to have bragging rights when it comes to their boarding abilities. Competitions are the way to do that.

RIGHT GUARD

or sheer guts and glory some of the most exciting competitions to watch are the Winter X Games, the Gravity Games, and Vans Triple Crown. Here's what's involved.

BIG AIR

The trick in a big-air competition is to explode down the hill, hit the takeoff point, try to go "huge" while pulling off a really difficult move, then stick the landing. Twenty-four men and 24 women compete one by one. Riders get three runs and are judged on four things—how high they go, how much distance they travel, how hard their trick is, and how perfect their landing is.

SLOPESTYLE

Take freeriding and add in a dose of jibbing. Mix in a competitive atmosphere on a slope outfitted with rails, picnic tables, mailboxes, obstacles, and a big gap. It all adds up to an awesome event. Riders get three runs each and are scored on style, amplitude, execution, originality, and how cleverly they cover the course.

SUPERPIPE

Bigger pipes mean more difficult combinations of tricks with double grabs and inverted spins. Twenty-four men and 24 women get three runs, showing off their slickest and most original moves.

SNOWBOARDER-X

Boardercross is called Snowboarder-X in the X Games. Riders charge down a hill in groups of six, elbowing one another around and over all sorts of obstacles—even jumping over a 60-foot gap to reach the finish line first. Speed *and* smarts will win this event.

HERE COMES THE JUDGE!

Some competitions are decided by a clock. But sometimes the winner is chosen by people who decide who did the best tricks with the most style. Meet the judges.

In a halfpipe contest, there are usually two sets of judges—a group at the top and a group at the bottom. Boarders are judged on five things:

1. AMPLITUDE: How many feet above the coping the rider flew. Some can soar almost ten feet.

2. LANDINGS: Smooth and in control, or messy.

3. GRABS: How many, and how hard.

4. SPINNING: The degree of difficulty and number of spins.

5. OVERALL IMPRESSION: How original the rider's routine was, how big the moves were.

Riders get a maximum of ten points for each category. A 50 is a perfect score.

Another event is the Jam Format. Instead of having just a few runs, riders squeeze as many runs as they can fit into an hour and a half—lots more opportunities to dazzle the judges.

Prize money is a sweet reward!

The Olympics

In 1998 something great happened in Nagano, Japan. As athletes from all over the world gathered to compete in the Winter Olympics, a new sport—yup, you guessed it, snowboarding— burst onto the scene.

Gearing up for the Olympics, American snowboarder Jimi Scott nails a handplant during a FIS World Cup halfpipe competition.

Who will get to compete in the next Winter Olympics? Who will wear the shimmering gold medal as his or her national anthem plays? And what events will leave us breathless as we watch the riders pushing themselves to new and astonishing limits?

Each participating country can send up to four boarders to the Olympics to compete in two snowboarding events—the giant slalom and halfpipe.

THE HALFPIPE EVENT

Thirty-five men and 20 women will stand at the entrance to the Olympic halfpipe with hearts hammering and knees knocking. They'll each begin with a preliminary round of two runs. Five judges score the boarders based on their technique, spins, amplitude, landings, and the difficulty of the tricks. After the first run, the four women and eight men with the highest scores will go on to the finals.

A second run pits the remaining boarders (16 women and 27 men) against each other. The highest ranked four women and eight men go on to the finals. Everyone else goes home.

In the final round the preliminary scores are tossed out and the boarders get two runs. The highest score gets the glory…and the gold.

GIANT SLALOM GLORY

Thirty-five men and 30 women will wait at the starting gates for this one-day event that sends them down two different runs. Every boarder races twice, and the winner will be the one with the lowest combined time. Miss one gate and you're out of the medal race. Nail them all in the fastest time and take home a shiny medal.

DO THE BEST BOARDERS END UP AT THE OLYMPICS?

Not always. The International Olympic Committee (IOC) picked the FIS (remember…this is basically a skier's organization) to be the group that ran qualifying events for the Olympics.

Most boarders, especially in the U.S., prefer the events run by the International Snowboard Federation. They believe that the IOC/skiing-backed FIS system does not have the best interests of the boarders or the sport in mind.

Most of the FIS competitions are held in faraway places and often conflict with important ISF events—such as the U.S. Open. Boarders have to choose between being seen in high-profile televised events where tons of fans have gathered, or traveling to somewhere really off-the-beaten-path.

To get to the Olympics, athletes often have to miss major ISF events—events that draw huge crowds and great publicity—to earn FIS points. And for a person who depends on money from a sponsor, such as a snowboard manufacturer, being seen is sometimes more important than getting points.

Extreme Sports

....

Part Four

The Legends

- **Great Beginnings**
- **Great Feats**

Inventors, dreamers, doers...
meet some of the most
amazing snowboarders
in the world.

Great Beginnings

People have been sliding across the snow on skis for thousands of years. Snowboards have been around for less than 40 years. But what wild and crazy years those have been!

Way back in 1966, a fellow named Sherman Poppen had a wacky idea. He took a piece of wood and nailed it to two skis, building a sled that you could ride standing up instead of sitting down. His kids loved it. So did the company he worked for. They took his little backyard toy, called it the Snurfer, and started selling it for ten bucks.

But not only little kids liked it. Some grown-ups thought it was pretty cool, too. Surfers loved it. Skateboarders loved it. And all it needed were a few little improvements....

Fun. But you need an ocean.

Neat. But you need a mountain.

Gassy. But you need a bobsled run (and 3 other guys).

Special offer!
Get your own pair of S-s-s-snurfing Goggles. Just $1 with purchase of Brunswick Snurfer. See dealer for details.

Wild. All you need is a little snow.

The Snurfer
BY BRUNSWICK.

Rides like a surfboard. Maneuvers like a ski. You can even sit on it like a sled. And you don't need a big hill or a lot of snow either. Ask for the original Snurfer by Brunswick. Standard or racing models, under $10.

BOYS' LIFE • DECEMBER, 1969

THE BLOCKHOUSE RACES

In 1968, after hiking almost a mile uphill to get to the race course, die-hard snurfers duked it out for bragging rights to the title "fastest snurfer." Two years later, a fellow named Dimitrije Milovich began to develop and patent a better kind of snurfer—made with a foam core and fiberglass skin. He called them Wintersticks.

MEANWHILE... DOWN IN NEW JERSEY

When Tom Sims was in middle school in 1963, he went to California and fell head over heels in love with skateboarding. But back home in New Jersey hardly anyone knew what a skateboard was, and Tom got a lot of weird looks when he returned.

When winter...and the snow...came, Tom's skateboard began to gather dust. So he decided to make a "ski board" in his 8th grade woodshop class. Tom's project was a piece of pine 8 inches wide, 12 inches long, and 3/4 inches thick. He fashioned a nose kick in the front. Carpet and strips of wood were glued to the top for traction, and candle wax and aluminum sheeting were layered onto the base. Soon Tom was catching small air at the local sled hill. Fourteen years later, in 1977, a grown-up Tom opened Sims Snowboards—and became one of the world's great board makers.

BETTER BOARDING

No one person can really take the credit for making snowboarding completely cool. But there are several people whose names became household words.

Take Jake Burton Carpenter. Jake snurfed for the first time when he was 14, broke a finger, but still loved it! Over the next few years he skied a lot and dreamed of becoming a member of the University of Colorado ski team. But as classes began, Jake managed to break his collarbone three times in two weeks, never made the team, and returned back East after a year. He tried exercising racehorses, then enrolled in another college. But the snow kept calling, so he took some money he had inherited, moved to Vermont, and began Burton Boards. Jake did it all himself, from cutting the boards to putting on the coats of urethane. He drove cross-country selling his board, answered the phone in the middle of the night to take orders, and worked tirelessly to make a great snowboard. Today Burton Boards are legendary.

And let's not forget Chuck Barfoot who created the first all-fiberglass snowboard back in 1978. He would make another huge snowboarding leap with the symmetrical twin-tip board ten years later. And boarding would never be the same!

Great Feats

There is a mountain on the other side of the world that reaches more than five miles into the sky. Hundreds have died trying to climb to its top. Now, imagine snowboarding down!

Everest is the world's tallest peak. People dream of climbing it, and more than 150 people have died making the ascent. Most people want to go *up*. But leave it to a snowboarder to size up this mega-mountain and decide to make a mark by going *down*.

Snowboarders are a do-their-own-thing kind of group. There have been boarders who've traveled to the heart of Africa to board, and those who face even greater challenges right in their own backyards.

On Mt. Everest—the mother of all mountains—winds often reach hurricane force. There are only a few weeks during the year when a trip to the top is possible.

TO EVEREST AND BEYOND

On May 22, 2001, a little bit of mountain-history was made. A snowboarder named Stefan Gatt did something amazing. Stefan climbed to the top of Mt. Everest—the world's tallest mountain. That would be difficult enough, but then Stefan strapped on his board and came straight down!

He was the first person to pull this off. And most amazingly, he did it all without using any bottled oxygen to help him breathe. The peak of Everest is more than five miles up, and there is hardly any oxygen in the air. A person dropped on the tip-top of the mountain would be dead in 20 minutes. To get to the top and survive, you have to go up very slowly, stopping for days at a time to allow your body to get used to the low-oxygen air. Very few people can climb Everest. Even fewer can do it without oxygen. And no one, until now, had ever boarded down.

NO MOUNTAIN TOO HIGH OR TOO STEEP

One of the greatest dreams of a mountaineer is getting to the top of the highest peak on each and every continent. One boarder has made it his goal to board down all of them! His name is Stephen Koch, and he has boarded down some of the biggest mountains on the planet. He dreamed up a "Seven Summit Snowboarding Quest" and began his mission in 1993 by climbing and then boarding down Mt. Aconcagua in Argentina. Later that year, Koch headed for Mt. McKinley, North America's highest peak. Since then, he has ridden Africa's Kilimanjaro, Europe's Mt. El'brus, and Antarctica's Vinson Massif. He has even taken his board to Indonesia to board down the highest peak on the the island of New Guinea, a place not known for its snow. Only Everest awaits to make his dream a reality.

Africa's Kilimanjaro slices through the clouds.

INNER MOUNTAINS

Sometimes, the greatest challenge in snowboarding isn't riding down a huge mountain. For boarders with disabilities—people who have lost arms and legs, people who cannot see—tackling a small mountain can be as hard as boarding down Everest. But the joy of ripping down the slopes can still be theirs. Some adaptive riders use outriggers to help them balance. Others use special prostheses (artificial arms and legs) to help them board. In time, snowboarding will become a paralympic sport—an event for disabled athletes that runs along with the Olympics.

Get Smart

- **Behavior**
- **Equipment**
- **Conditioning**
- **Resources**

Oh, Behave!

Manners, manners! Most boarders are actually very well-behaved. But just in case you weren't sure, here are some dos and don'ts.

oving down the mountain at 50 miles an hour is thrilling. It can also be really dangerous. One out-of-control skier actually did prison time after his recklessness led to the death of another person on the mountain. So, here comes the lecture…but it's a lecture that could save your life.

SLOPESIDE SAFETY

For a long time, boarders had a reputation for being wild and disrespectful. It has taken years to get people to drop that stereotype. It's up to you to keep it that way. Let common sense rule! If you see a person boarding like a bully, let someone from the ski patrol or the ski area know.

And as for you…here are a few things to keep in mind.
• Make sure your board has a runaway strap on it. Getting decked with a flying board can be deadly.
• Know the different trail markings. Don't let your friends talk you into trying a run that's way beyond your ability. If you are not an expert, you are not magically going to become one because your buddies are.
• And most importantly, if a trail is marked closed, it means IT'S CLOSED! It's stupid and dangerous to ignore the warning signs.

TERRAIN PARK TIPS

A few "words to the wise" for those of you who use terrain parks. Only *you* know your ability. Don't attempt anything that scares you. Be aware of the weather and over-use changes. Icy patches can be a real bummer. NEVER stop on the landing areas. Keep moving and be careful!

REMEMBER THESE …OR STAY HOME!

These are the basic rules every rider MUST follow.

1. Before riding the lifts, make sure you know how to get on and off safely.

2. You should always be in complete control of your board. Make sure you can stop or avoid other people or objects. If you can't, you don't belong on the mountain.

3. Remember that the people ahead of you have the right-of-way. It is your job not to hit them. It is NOT their job to get out of your way.

4. Never stop where you block a trail or are not visible from higher up on the slope.

5. Whenever you are starting downhill or merging with another trail, slow down and look uphill. You have to yield to others already on their way down.

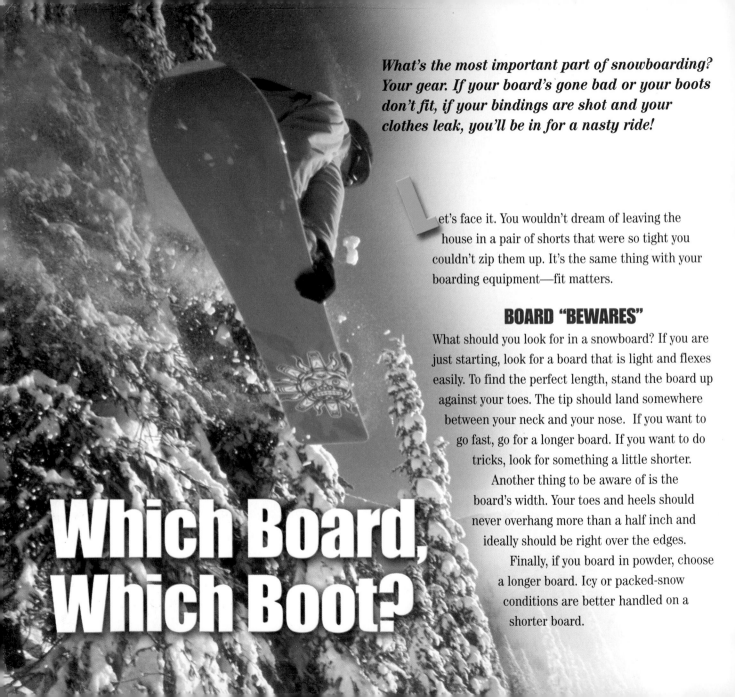

What's the most important part of snowboarding? Your gear. If your board's gone bad or your boots don't fit, if your bindings are shot and your clothes leak, you'll be in for a nasty ride!

Let's face it. You wouldn't dream of leaving the house in a pair of shorts that were so tight you couldn't zip them up. It's the same thing with your boarding equipment—fit matters.

BOARD "BEWARES"

What should you look for in a snowboard? If you are just starting, look for a board that is light and flexes easily. To find the perfect length, stand the board up against your toes. The tip should land somewhere between your neck and your nose. If you want to go fast, go for a longer board. If you want to do tricks, look for something a little shorter. Another thing to be aware of is the board's width. Your toes and heels should never overhang more than a half inch and ideally should be right over the edges.

Finally, if you board in powder, choose a longer board. Icy or packed-snow conditions are better handled on a shorter board.

Which Board, Which Boot?

BOOT CAMP

Your boots are your most important piece of equipment. They have to fit right. There are two basic kinds of boot—soft and hard. Soft boots are best for jibbing, riding the pipes, and freeriding. Hard boots are a must for speed events and are rarely used for halfpipe or jibbing. Nowadays there is also a soft-hard combo boot for high-performance boarding.

Soft boots have an inner bladder that is thick and cushy. They should feel a little snug when you try them on. Make sure your heels don't slide around. Hard boots, which look like ski boots, should fit more snugly. You want them to be stiff since they have to keep you from wiping out when you go for those hard turns.

STEP IN OR BUCKLE UP

Bindings hold your boots to your board. Highback bindings will clamp soft boots to the board with two or three buckles. Step-in bindings were inspired by ski bindings…easy to get in and out of but sometimes not as comfortable as straps. Alpinists use plate bindings to firmly hold their boots in place. There's nothing worse than popping out of your binding when you're rounding a gate.

The choice of step-in or strap-on bindings and soft or hard boots is a very personal one. If you can, rent each type and decide, slopeside, which suits you best.

CARING FOR YOUR GEAR

A cared-for board will do what you tell it to, turning smoothly, the edges gripping as you ride. Even if you're just a beginner, you'll move much better with a well-tuned board.

1. KEEP YOUR BOARD WELL WAXED—Wax makes your board slip over the snow more smoothly. It's fairly easy to do once you know how (always with a little help from an adult).

2. DRY YOUR BOOTS PROPERLY— Don't let your boots dry open. The materials your boots are made of have a "memory." If you leave them unbuckled they will dry and stiffen in an open position.

Caring for Yourself

No self-respecting snowboarder would dare to hit the slopes without being in really tip-top shape. And the really great snowboarders work out almost every single day. They eat right. They get lots of sleep. And they have a few secrets to help them fly higher!

Every Olympic snowboarder knows it. The winners at the X Games swear by it. If you want to get good at snowboarding, you've got to spend a lot of time on a trampoline.

During the summer months, when snow is nothing but a distant memory, most serious riders can be found, drenched in sweat, working on their grabs. They do it by jumping on big trampolines, bouncing for hours every day. They do *not* goof around. They do *not* try dangerous stunts. They are always extremely careful.

KEEPING IN SHAPE

Boarders who specialize in riding halfpipes or terrain parks in winter will hop on their skateboards come spring. Most drop in to the nearest skate park to keep their skills sharp. You can't be a top rider if you only do it a few months a year. If you're a serious snowboarder, you should definitely skateboard since many snowboarding moves were picked up from skateboarders.

CAMP SNOW

For die-hard boarders summer doesn't have to mean the end of riding. There are quite a few camps in North America where year-round white stuff makes for radical riding. Some camps are run on glaciers, huge masses of slow-creeping ice and snow that form in places where more snow falls than can melt. And since it's summer, kids sometimes get to practice their inverts and spins by landing in a swimming pool! (See page 64 for a list of camps.)

THREE BOUNCES TO GREATNESS

Here's a fitness exercise that a lot of top boarders do. But before you try it, swear that you will follow common-sense safety on the trampoline. Remember… only one jumper at a time, and make sure a grown-up is around. And don't forget to stretch before you start.

1. Jump up and down as high as you can—slowly and steadily getting higher.

2. Bring your knees up to your chest on each jump.

3. Now, land flat on your back, legs stretched out, hands at your side.

4. Next, spring up and land face down, flat on your stomach, then land on your feet.

5. Then for your next move, do a somersault, landing on your feet.

6. The goal is to do the three moves in a smooth, effortless fashion with no breaks between. You should be able to go from back to front without stopping.

Practice whenever you can. Think snowboarding. Dream snowboarding. Breathe snowboarding. And know that if you can dream it, you can probably make it happen!

To Find Out More...

SNOWBOARDING MAGAZINES

SNOWBOARDING AND SNOWBOARD LIFE
www.snowboarding-online.com
This is an excellent site with all sorts of information—even Quicktime video instructions on the newest moves.

SNOWBOARDER
www.snowboardermag.com

SNOWBOARDING ORGANIZATIONS

INTERNATIONAL SNOWBOARD FEDERATION
(ISF) OF NORTH AMERICA
315 Fergus Falls, MN 56537
www.snowboardranking.com

UNITED STATES OF AMERICA SNOWBOARD
ASSOCIATION (USASA)
P.O. Box 3927
Truckee, CA 96160
www.usasa.org

CANADIAN SKI AND SNOWBOARD ASSOCIATION
305 - 2197 Riverside Drive
Ottawa, ON, Canada, K1H 7X3
www.canadaskiandsnowboard.net

SNOWBOARDING CAMPS

HIGH CASCADE SNOWBOARD CAMP
P.O. Box 6622, Bend, Oregon 97708
www.highcascade.com

MT. HOOD SNOWBOARD CAMP
P.O. Box 140, Rhododendron, Oregon 97049
www.snowboardcamp.com

WHISTLER SUMMER SNOWBOARD CAMP
103-4338 Main St., Suite 981
Whistler, BC, Canada V0N 1B4
www.whistlersnowboardcamps.com

PRO RIDE SNOWBOARD CAMPS
103-4338 Main St., Suite 963
Whistler, BC, Canada V0N 1B4
www.pro-ride.com

WINDELL'S SNOWBOARD CAMP
P.O. Box 628 Welches, OR 97067
www.windells.com

SPECIAL PROGRAM

CHILL: THE BURTON FOUNDATION
Chill is a national non-profit learn-to-snowboard program for at-risk inner-city kids between the ages of 10 and 18. Operating out of 8 hub cities, it offers six-week all-expenses paid programs for disadvantaged youths.
www.burton.com/the_company/about_chill.asp

PHOTO CREDITS

Scott Serfas: Pages 22, 23, 30, 50-51, 56-57, 60, back cover, large photo. Jean-Francois Vibert: Pages 4-5, 26, 40. Mike Ponte/Ponteography: Pages 12, 13, 24, 25, 31, 41, 46. Mike Piniewski/ Frost Hollow Photography: Pages 16, 20, 44, 47. Burton Snowboards: Pages 32, 61 top. Corbis: Pages 18-19, 42-43, 48. Tony Stone: Page 58. Image State: Page 6. Photodisc: cover, Pages 2-3, 10, 14, 27, 55, 61, bottom, 63. Corbis Royalty Free: Pages 7, 15, 21, 59, 62. Eyewire: Pages 8-9. Digital Vision: Pages 34, 36, 38, 62.The Stock Market: Page 10. Bill Marsh: Pages 26-27.Weststock: Page 54

THE AUTHOR THANKS...

This book would have been impossible to create without the help of Tertius Bune, whose knowledge of, and passion for, snowboarding made for a thrilling ride!

Thanks also to...
- *Scott Serfas, Mike Ponte, Jean-Francois Vibert, and Michael Piniewski whose beautiful photographs captured all the excitement of the sport.*
- *Tina Basich for her expertise.*
- *Alex Scolnik for his contributions to the production of Snowboard!*
- *Burton Snowboards for their help and cooperation.*

Library of Congress
Cataloging-in-Publication Data
Masoff, Joy, 1951—
Snowboard ! / by Joy Masoff
p. cm. —(Extreme Sports)
Includes bibliographical references
(p.) and index.
Summary: Describes different kinds of snow-boarding—freeriding, in the pipe, jibbling, backcountry—and the techniques, equipment, and terminology involved.
ISBN 0-7922-6740-0 (pbk.)
1. Snowboarding—Juvenile literature.
[1. Snowboarding.] I. Title. II. Extreme sports
(Washington, D.C.)
GV857.S57 M353 2002   796.93'9—dc21
                                        2001044392